No, I and **Bedtime**

PHASE 2

/ck/e/u/
r/h/b/
f/

Level 2 – Red

Helpful Hints for Reading at Home

The graphemes (written letters) and phonemes (units of sound) used throughout this series are aligned with Letters and Sounds. This offers a consistent approach to learning whether reading at home or in the classroom.

HERE IS A LIST OF PHONEMES FOR THIS PHASE OF LEARNING. AN EXAMPLE OF THE PRONUNCIATION CAN BE FOUND IN BRACKETS.

Phase 2			
s (sat)	a (cat)	t (tap)	p (tap)
i (pin)	n (net)	m (man)	d (dog)
g (go)	o (sock)	c (cat)	k (kin)
ck (sack)	e (elf)	u (up)	r (rabbit)
h (hut)	b (ball)	f (fish)	ff (off)
l (lip)	ll (ball)	ss (hiss)	

HERE ARE SOME WORDS WHICH YOUR CHILD MAY FIND TRICKY.

Phase 2 Tricky Words			
the	to	I	no
go	into		

GPC focus: /ck/e/u/r/h/b/f/

TOP TIPS FOR HELPING YOUR CHILD TO READ:

• Allow children time to break down unfamiliar words into units of sound and then encourage children to string these sounds together to create the word.

• Encourage your child to point out any focus phonics when they are used.

• Read through the book more than once to grow confidence.

• Ask simple questions about the text to assess understanding.

• Encourage children to use illustrations as prompts.

PHASE 2

/ck/e/u/ r/h/b/ f/

This book focuses on the phonemes /ck/, /e/, /u/, /r/, /h/, /b/ and /f/ and is a red level 2 book band.

No, Rin!
and
Bedtime

Written by
Madeline Tyler

Illustrated by
Danielle Webster-Jones

Can you say this sound and draw it with your finger?

No, Rin!

Written by
Madeline Tyler

Illustrated by
Danielle Webster-Jones

Ron and Rick and Rin.

Ron and Rick. "Back to us, Rin!"

"Rin, get a peg!"

"Can I get a carrot?"
"No, Rin!"

"Rin, get a hat!"

"Can I get a carrot?"
"No, Rin!"

"Rin, get a sock!"

"Can I get a carrot?"
"No, Rin!"

Rin is sad.
"Back to us, Rin!"

"It is sad."

"Can I get a carrot?"
"Yes, Rin!"

It is fun! It is not sad!

Can you say this sound and draw it with your finger?

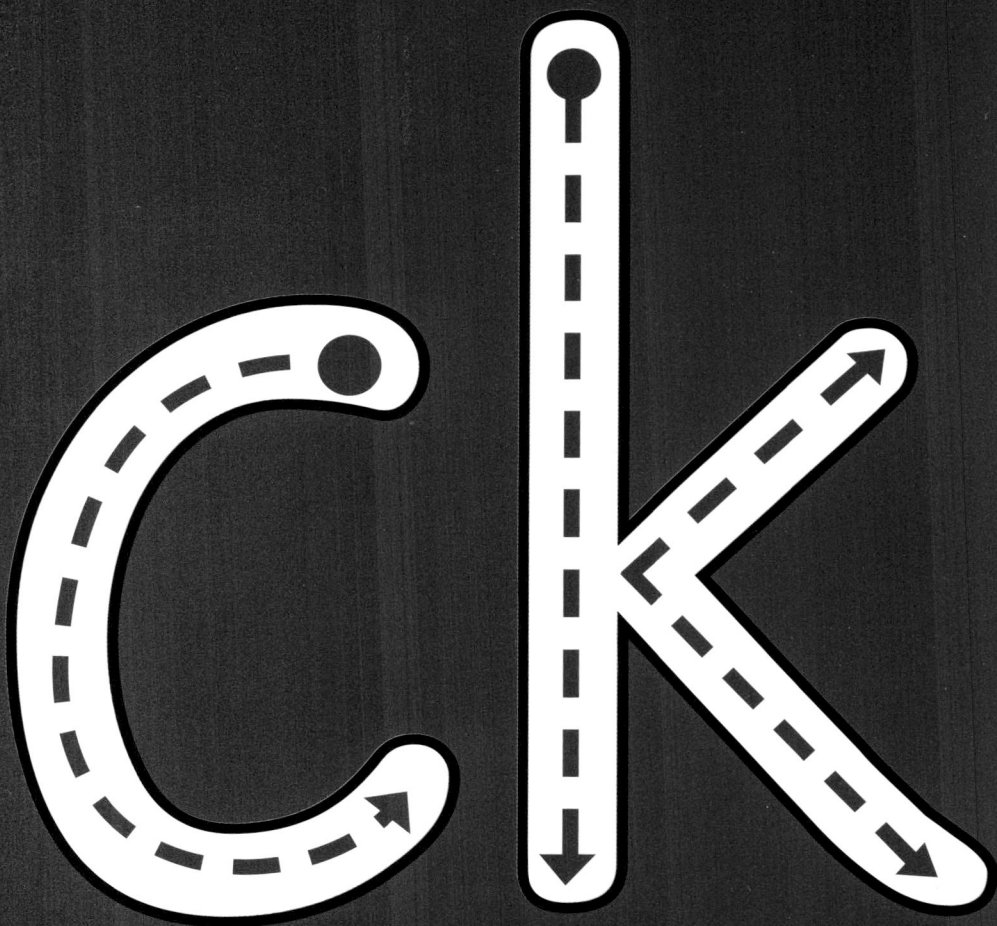

c k

Bedtime

Written by
Madeline Tyler

Illustrated by
Danielle Webster-Jones

Tuck Ron up in bed.

Tuck Rick up in bed.

Tuck Rin up in bed.

"It is a rocket, not a bed!"

A big, red, bed rocket!

Ron, Rick and Rin in a rocket.

"It is a big sock, not a rocket!"

Ron, Rick and Rin in a sock.

"It is a den, not a sock!"

Ron, Rick and Rin in a den.

Back to bed. But Mum and Ma Ma!

Tuck Mum and Ma Ma up in bed.

BookLife
PUBLISHING

BookLife
Readers

©2021 **BookLife Publishing Ltd.**
King's Lynn, Norfolk PE30 4LS

ISBN 978-1-83927-430-5

No, Rin! and Bedtime
Written by Madeline Tyler
Illustrated by Danielle Webster-Jones

An Introduction to BookLife Readers...

Our Readers have been specifically created in line with the London Institute of Education's approach to book banding and are phonetically decodable and ordered to support each phase of Letters and Sounds.

Each book has been created to provide the best possible reading and learning experience. Our aim is to share our love of books with children, providing both emerging readers and prolific page-turners with beautiful books that are guaranteed to provoke interest and learning, regardless of ability.

BOOK BAND GRADED using the Institute of Education's approach to levelling.

PHONETICALLY DECODABLE supporting each phase of Letters and Sounds.

EXERCISES AND QUESTIONS to offer reinforcement and to ascertain comprehension.

BEAUTIFULLY ILLUSTRATED to inspire and provoke engagement, providing a variety of styles for the reader to enjoy whilst reading through the series.

AUTHOR INSIGHT:
MADELINE TYLER

Native to Norfolk, England, Madeline Tyler's intelligence and professionalism can be felt in the 50-plus books that she has written for BookLife Publishing. A graduate of Queen Mary University of London with a 1st Class degree in Comparative Literature, she also received a University Volunteering Award for helping children to read at a local school.

When she was a child, Madeline enjoyed playing the violin, and she now relaxes through yoga and reading books!

PHASE 2
/ck/e/u/ r/h/b/ f/

This book focuses on the phonemes /ck/, /e/, /u/, /r/, /h/, /b/ and /f/ and is a red level 2 book band.